# Praise for **Heroes!**
## and the *Rainbow Reach Series*

"As a licensed clinical psychologist, with several years of experience helping children with the issues contained in the *Rainbow Reach Series*, I would utilize the books in a child's therapy to help them learn how to express difficult thoughts and feelings. The books are colorful, engaging, and easy to use, and the activities will help children address the impact of life events in healthy ways."

Lynn J. Piper, Ph.D., LCP
Animal Assisted and Trauma Therapist

"The *Rainbow Reach Series* is wonderful! I love the way that a child's creativity is utilized in identifying emotions and focusing on blessings. The books offer excellent yet simple text and drive the lessons of optimism, acceptance of feelings and resilience home in truly age-appropriate ways. Bravo!"

Fran Zamore, MSW, ACSW
Author of: *GriefWork – Healing from Loss* and
*The GriefWork Companion – Activities for Healing*
Bereavement Coordinator, Holy Cross Hospice – Silver Spring, MD
Private Practice

"In an age of communication by social media networks, Twitter, Facebook, and other non-physically connected devices, it is refreshing to find a means to help children deal with the pain of loss, parental deployment, worry and anxiety that is non-electronic and allows for multimedia expression of feelings in an interactive format. The use of drawings and activities illustrate more complex concepts such as projection, desensitization, grief, mourning, and guilt. The *Heroes!* activity book is an excellent tool for children whose parent or parents are being deployed in dangerous, life-threatening war zones. Without dwelling on the negative impacts of deployment, this workbook approaches deployment from the positive of what the hero parent is doing to help our country and how those children can preserve a long-distance relationship."

Mary Beth Williams, Ph.D., LCSW
Trauma Recovery and Education Counseling Center

(continued)

"Children heal best when they are engaged in activities that help them express and resolve difficult feelings. The *Rainbow Reach Series* provides such activities in a creative, interesting workbook format that will help children move beyond grief and anxiety."

Mary W. Lindahl, Ph.D.
Professor of Psychology, Marymount University
Licensed Clinical Psychologist

"Susan Weaver has created the *Rainbow Reach Series* as a comprehensive tool for children to express thoughts and feelings involving death and loss. From pet loss, to worry, deployment and death, these interactive workbooks create the safe space for expression so needed for our bereaved girls and boys. Parents and professionals will assuredly benefit from using these resources to develop communication and sharing, and normalize a child's grief journey. The *Rainbow Reach Series* is a valuable tool for young people and adults to use in recognizing the multifaceted aspects of grieving, and for supporting outlooks for recovery and resilience that can be useful throughout a lifetime."

Linda Goldman, Grief Therapist and Educator
Author of: *Life and Loss, Children Also Grieve*, and *Raising Our Children to Be Resilient*

Praise for other books in the *Rainbow Reach Series*

# Worry Busters!

"I particularly like the *Worry Busters!* activity that helps children decide how <u>big</u> their worry is and how to make their worry smaller."

Nancy S. Price, LCSW – Licensed Clinical Social Worker

# Forever Friend

"Over the years as a veterinarian, I have been asked how to help children work through the loss of a family pet. In the small world of a child, a family pet occupies more of that world than we adults may understand. This book provides a tool to help our children work through what they may be feeling in the loss of a pet they cherished. The "doing" activity focus of the book provides a tactile venue to help spark heart to heart communication, which is essential in the healing process."

Andrew Voell, DVM – Pender Veterinary Centre – Fairfax, VA

# HEROES!

## Activities for Kids Dealing with Deployment

by Susan B. Weaver

Published by:

www.rainbowreach.com

Rainbow Reach
Post Office Box 461
Herndon, VA 20172-0461 U.S.A.
www.rainbowreach.com

Other books in the **Rainbow Reach Series...**

Forever Friend: *Activities for Kids Who Have Lost a Pet*

Love & Memories: *Activities for Kids Who Have Lost a Loved One*

Worry Busters! *Activities for Kids Who Worry Too Much*

Weaver, Susan B.
Heroes! *Activities for Kids Dealing with Deployment*
SUMMARY: A book to help children cope with the separation of having a parent or
loved one deployed. Includes drawing and writing activities that enable a
child's feelings to be expressed.
Audience: Ages 4-14

Printed in the United States of America on Acid-Free Paper

10 9 8 7 6 5 4 3 2 1

ISBN: 978-0-9829490-2-3

Library of Congress Control Number: 2011920725

1. Children. 2. Military. 3. Deployment.

# A Note to Grown-Ups

Children with deployed parents or loved ones face a different set of issues, worry, and anxiety than other children. Living on a military base or installation can help, due to a structured support system, but all of these children face the circumstance of missing a parent or loved one, and it's often difficult for them to rationalize or understand the reason this person is gone.

It's important for these children to know that the person who is deployed loves and misses them ... that their loved one has been trained to do an important job, and that's what he or she will be doing. At the same time, these children need the security of knowing that they will be taken care of and loved in the absence of the person who is deployed.

Talking about their thoughts and feelings, and expressing their concerns, will help children get questions answered and reassure them that everything is ok. A structured schedule will keep kids busy, and knowing how to relax can help calm their nerves. Confirmation that they are not alone in their concerns can also be a great comfort.

Young children will need a good deal of assistance completing these activities. They may not understand why the deployed person is gone, but talking about it and getting questions answered can be a big help.

Older children will be able to complete the activities on their own but may still welcome your love and assurance. By setting an example of how YOU feel, you can show kids that it's ok (and healthy) to express their own feelings and emotions.

## Color these pages!

Completing the activities and coloring the pages in this book will serve as a wonderful tribute to the Hero who is temporarily away, and will create a joyful display of love to share upon his or her return.

# WHAT IS DEPLOYMENT?

Deployment is when someone has to go away to do his or her job. Sometimes a person is deployed for long periods of time.

# WHAT IS A HERO?

A Hero is someone who defends his or her country and makes sacrifices in order for others to be safe and comfortable.

It is hard for your HERO to be away from you – your HERO misses you just as much as you miss him or her.

# WHO IS YOUR HERO?

## Who is deployed? My:

☆ Dad      ☆ Stepdad

☆ Mom      ☆ Aunt

☆ Brother      ☆ Uncle

☆ Sister      ☆ Cousin

☆ Stepmom      ☆ Friend

Someone Else? Who? _____

## Draw a picture of your Hero!

# Who else besides you is missing your Hero?

## Ask them to sign this Guest Page!

*Or fill in their names below.*

## Guests

_____

_____

_____

_____

_____

_____

They can share thoughts and stories...

And help fill in this book!

# In what branch of the Armed Forces does your Hero serve?

## UNITED STATES ARMED FORCES

Ask a grown-up to help you go online to see the correct colors...
www.rainbowreach.com/emblems.html

**ARMY**

**MARINE CORPS**

**NAVY**

**AIR FORCE**

**COAST GUARD**

# UNITED STATES NATIONAL GUARD

**ARMY NATIONAL GUARD**

NOT THE OFFICIAL
AIR NATIONAL GUARD SYMBOL

**AIR NATIONAL GUARD**

# UNITED STATES MILITARY RESERVE

**ARMY RESERVE**

**MARINE FORCES RESERVE**

**NAVY RESERVE**

**AIR FORCE RESERVE**

**COAST GUARD RESERVE**

# SERVING FROM ANOTHER COUNTRY?
## WHAT COUNTRY AND BRANCH OF SERVICE?

# Make up your own
## special patch for YOUR Hero!

Draw it on this page.

# Draw a picture of how much you love your Hero...

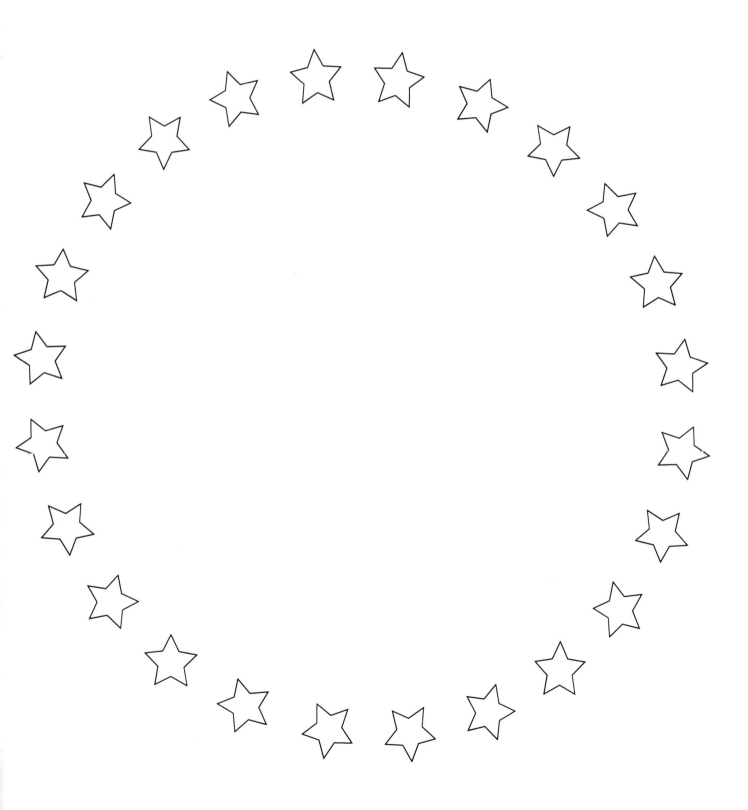

# Did you do something special with your Hero before he or she left on deployment?

As a family? _____

Just the two of you? _____

_____

_____

# Did you go with your Hero to say goodbye?

Yes [ ]     No [ ]

Was this the
best way
for you to
say goodbye?

(write your answer here)

GOODBYE

_____

_____

_____

_____

_____

_____

# Draw a picture of the last fun thing you did with your Hero before your Hero was deployed!

# Who can you ALWAYS depend on when your Hero is deployed?

Your Mom

Your Grandma

Your Grandpa

Your Stepmom

Your Dad

Your Stepdad

Your Aunt

Your Brother

Your Uncle

Your Sister

Someone else? Who?

Why don't you ask this person to help you fill in this book!

Do you wish you knew MORE or LESS about where your Hero is and what your Hero is doing?

More ☐    Less ☐

What do you wish you knew MORE about?

UPDATE

_____

_____

_____

_____

What do you wish you did NOT know and why?

NEWS

_____

_____

_____

_____

# How do you feel most of the time?

Ask someone what these feelings mean if you don't know them all.
It's ok to have more than one answer.

○ Pretty Good

○ Wonderful

○ Happy

○ Excited

○ Joyful

○ Thankful

○ Alert

○ Proud

○ Satisfied

○ Friendly

○ Loving

○ Energetic

○ Courageous

○ Trusting

○ Hopeful

○ Relaxed

○ Stressed

○ Worried

○ Angry

○ Mad

○ Anxious

○ Afraid

○ Helpless

○ Frustrated

○ Bored

○ Tense

○ Depressed

○ Lonely

○ Scared

○ Sad

○ Tired

○ Cranky

○ My feelings keep changing back and forth all the time.

# Draw pictures of how you feel...

For Example:

It's OK to feel sad, mad, lonely...or to change back and forth.

# It's good to let your feelings out!

It's a good idea to talk with a trusted grown-up about how you feel so you can work through your feelings.

Play sports.

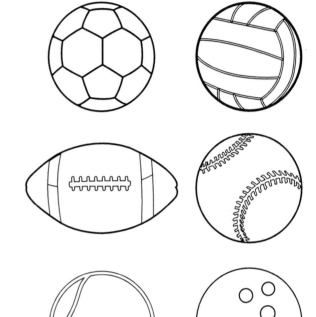

If you feel really mad or upset, here are some things that might help...

Play with a pet.

Go outside and
jump up and down
or run around!

Get some exercise!

Can you think of some things that may make you feel better?

_____   _____

_____   _____

_____   _____

_____

# How is your Hero's job different when he or she is deployed?

Helping people in other countries?

Building things?

Fighting in a war?

Being a leader?

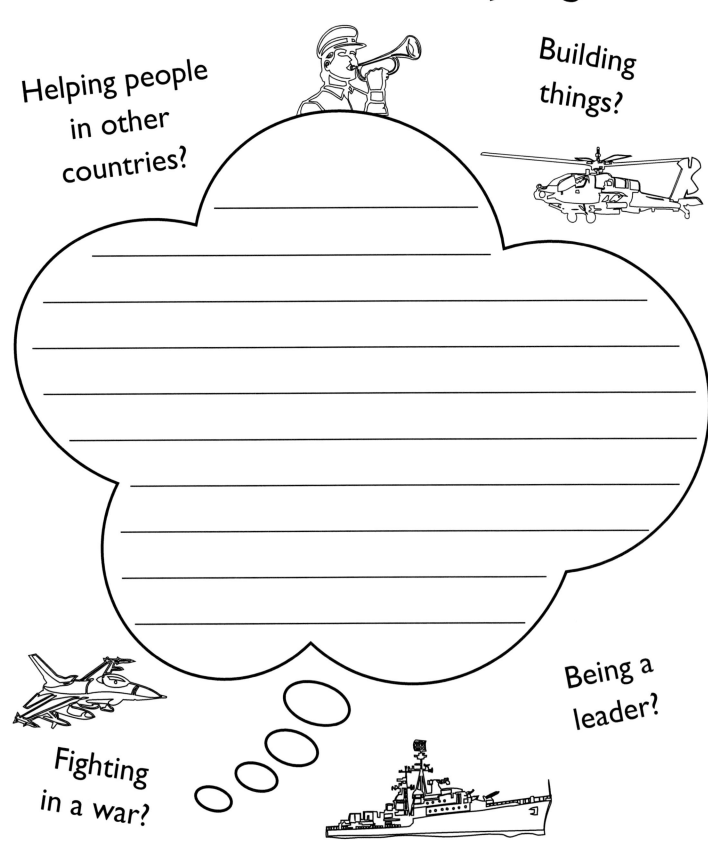

# Draw a picture of what your Hero has been trained to do in the military!

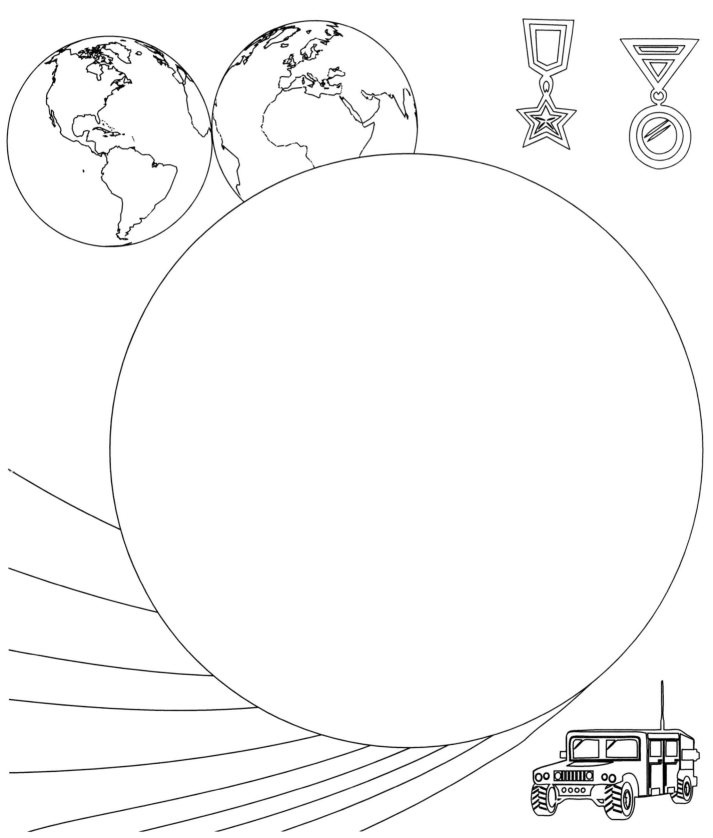

# How have things changed since your Hero was deployed?

## Do you have:

♡ A different schedule?

♡ More rules to follow?

♡ Less rules to worry about?

♡ More chores and responsibilities?

♡ People you have to take care of?

What else has changed since your Hero was deployed?

_____   _____

_____   _____

_____   _____

_____   _____

_____   _____

Things To Do:

Do you like these changes...and why or why not?

_____

_____

_____

_____

_____

_____

_____

# Do you feel different than your civilian friends who don't deal with deployment?

How are things different for you than for your civilian friends?

You have to move all the time and make new friends, and that can be really hard?

Do you feel like you know more about the world?

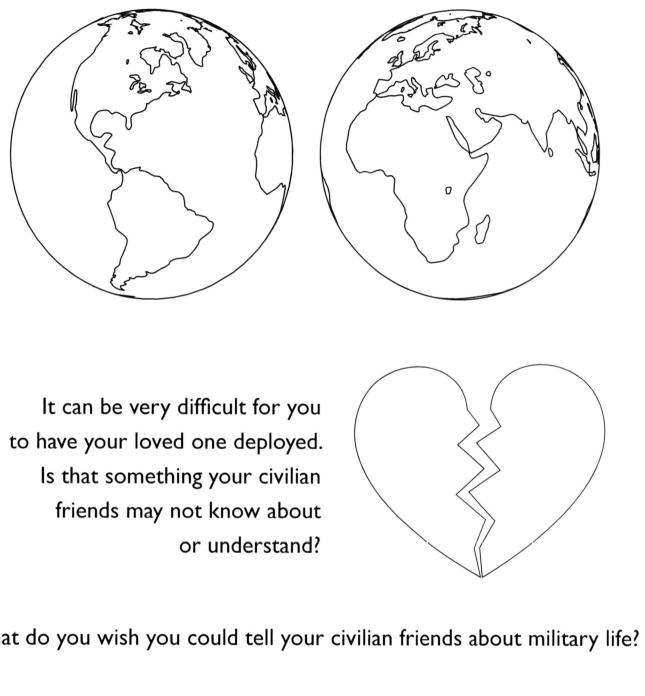

It can be very difficult for you
to have your loved one deployed.
Is that something your civilian
friends may not know about
or understand?

What do you wish you could tell your civilian friends about military life?

_____

_____

_____

_____

_____

# Frame pictures of your Hero!

1) Get some pictures of your Hero...
   (ask a grown-up what pictures you can use)

2) Place the pictures on these pages...
   (attach the pictures with glue or tape)

3) Color a frame around each picture!

draw your frame!

example

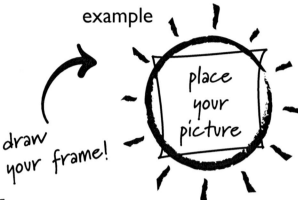

place your picture

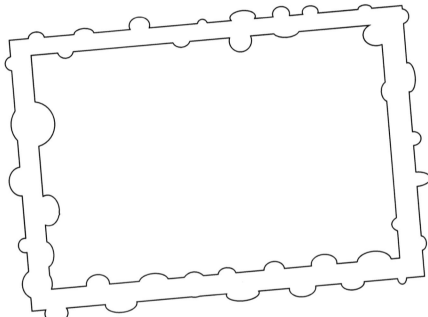

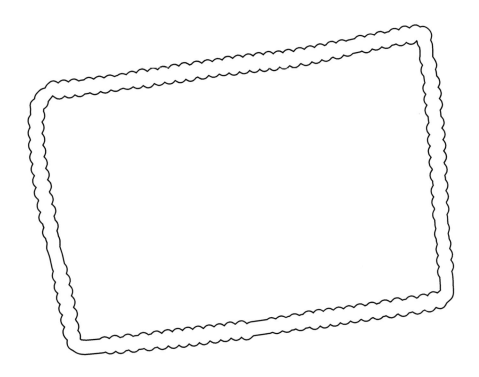

# Frame more pictures here!

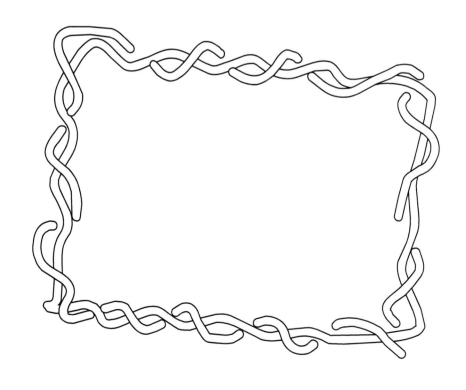

# What things make you feel better when you are missing your Hero?

Crossing Days Off the Calendar Until Your Hero Comes Home

Helping Others

Exercising

Days Until My Hero Comes Home

Keeping a Journal or Scrapbook to Show Your Hero When He or She Returns Home

Writing Daily or Weekly Postcards

Talking to Friends

# Write your own ideas!

Playing Games

Daydreaming

Relaxing

Being Around Other People

# What are your favorite things?

_____

_____

_____

_____

_____

_____

_____

_____

_____

_____

# Draw pictures of your MOST favorite things!

# What makes you feel happy?

_____

_____

_____

_____

_____

_____

_____

_____

_____

_____

# Draw pictures of what makes you happy!

# What can you do when you are sad or feel bad...

Play games
with your friends?

Hopscotch

Duck Duck Goose

Freeze Tag

Jacks

What are YOUR
favorite games?

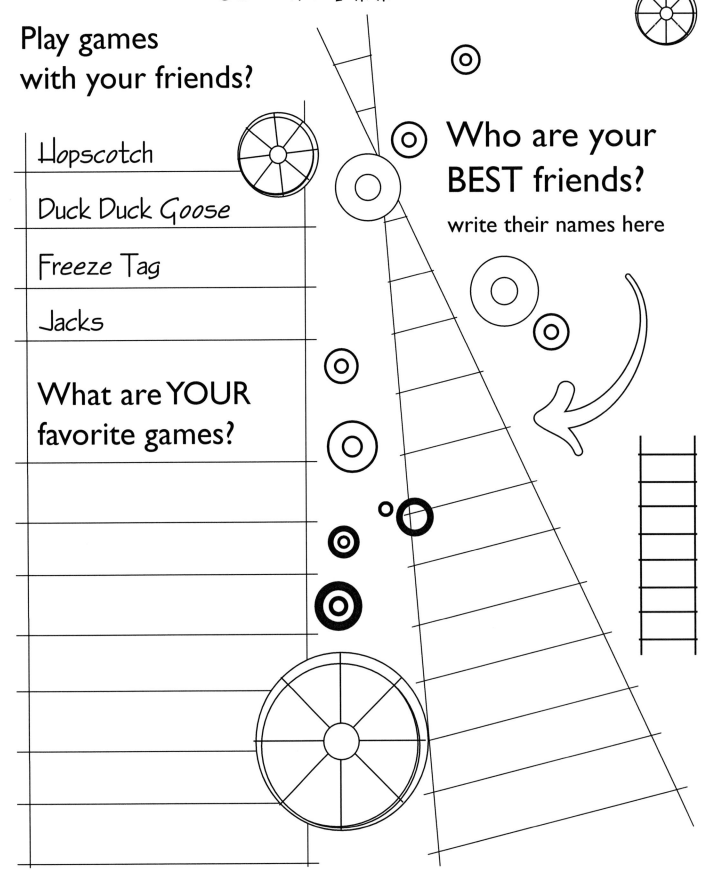

Who are your
BEST friends?

write their names here

# What else do you like to do?

Dance

Jump

Go to the Park

Play Video Games

List some things you really like to do...

_____   _____

_____   _____

_____   _____

_____   _____

# Try to Relax! Here are some FUN ways to relax...

## Spaghetti Toes*

Pretend you're a noodle! Imagine each part of your body is uncooked (stiff) spaghetti...and then cooked (soft) spaghetti. Start with your wriggly toes and make all the different parts of your body as soft as cooked spaghetti.

## Jelly Belly*

Take slow, deep breaths and watch how your stomach moves in and out. Try this when you're stressed and you will feel better and more relaxed right away, instead of getting more upset.

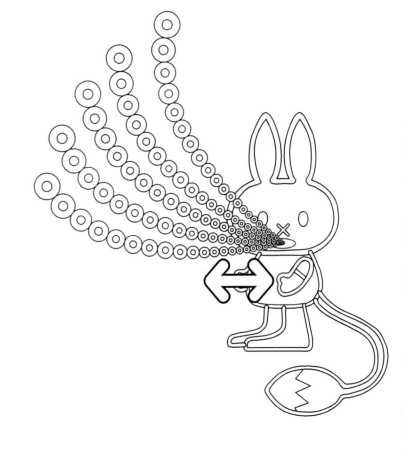

# Pleasant Park*

Pretend you're walking through a peaceful park in your mind, helping you feel calm and relaxed.

---

# Changing Channels*

If you don't like the mood you're in, change it by Changing Channels! Imagine holding a remote control, and click it to change to another mood (channel)!

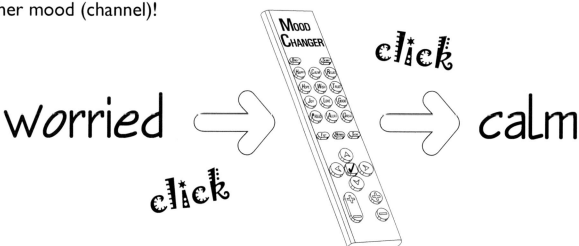

worried ➡ calm

click       click

---

## Ask a grown-up to look this up online to find out more!

\* These exercises and many others were developed by Dr. Terry Orlick to teach children and youth essential skills to enhance their learning, performance, and positive interactions with others. Go to www.rainbowreach.com/relax.html for more exercises along with matching soundtracks. Dr. Orlick's newest book: *Positive Living Skills – Joy and Focus for Everyone* can be found at www.zoneofexcellence.ca/index_new.html. All of Dr. Orlick's books, as well as his excellent series of relaxation CDs for children can be found at www.zoneofexcellence.ca/products_new.html#books. Dr. Orlick's books and CDs are also available at www.amazon.com.

# Draw a picture of yourself relaxing and having fun at the beach...

...or at the water park!

# Let's take a look at your schedule!

Are there times when you don't have stuff to do?

## During the School Year

|  | Monday - Friday | Saturday | Sunday |
|---|---|---|---|
| 6 am - 9 am | _____ | _____ | _____ |
|  | _____ | _____ | _____ |
| 9 am - 11 am | _____ | _____ | _____ |
|  | _____ | _____ | _____ |
| 11 am - 1 pm | _____ | _____ | _____ |
|  | _____ | _____ | _____ |
| 1 pm - 3 pm | _____ | _____ | _____ |
|  | _____ | _____ | _____ |
| 3 pm - 5 pm | _____ | _____ | _____ |
|  | _____ | _____ | _____ |
| 5 pm - 7 pm | _____ | _____ | _____ |
|  | _____ | _____ | _____ |
| 7 pm - Bedtime | _____ | _____ | _____ |
|  | _____ | _____ | _____ |

# Find times when you aren't busy and fill them in with things you like to do.

## During the Summer

|  | Monday - Friday | Saturday | Sunday |
|---|---|---|---|
| 6 am - 9 am | _____ | _____ | _____ |
|  | _____ | _____ | _____ |
| 9 am - 11 am | _____ | _____ | _____ |
|  | _____ | _____ | _____ |
| 11 am - 1 pm | _____ | _____ | _____ |
|  | _____ | _____ | _____ |
| 1 pm - 3 pm | _____ | _____ | _____ |
|  | _____ | _____ | _____ |
| 3 pm - 5 pm | _____ | _____ | _____ |
|  | _____ | _____ | _____ |
| 5 pm - 7 pm | _____ | _____ | _____ |
|  | _____ | _____ | _____ |
| 7 pm - Bedtime | _____ | _____ | _____ |
|  | _____ | _____ | _____ |

# You should be very proud of yourself...
# You are a Hero TOO!

For being strong and helping others whenever possible.

For helping to take care of your family.

For being nice
to others.

For doing things that make your life good even though parts of it are really hard.

By being proud of your Hero and doing the best you can while he or she is gone!

# What are some other things that would make your Hero super proud of you?

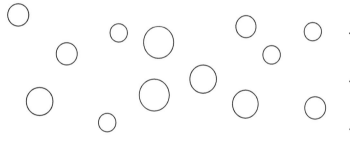

_____

_____

_____

_____

_____

_____

_____

_____

_____

_____

_____

_____

# Draw pictures of yourself doing these things!

# Write down some words that describe your Hero...

_____     _____

_____     _____

_____     _____

_____     _____

_____

Now make up a <u>story</u> or <u>poem</u> about your Hero using the words you wrote!

*You might want to ask for help on this one!*

My Hero is ...

_____

... and it will be wonderful to have my Hero home again!

# Write more stories or poems...

# What is your favorite song?

Write the name of the song here: _____

## Now write down the words as you sing the song.

Here are some suggestions if you cannot think of a song!

| | | |
|---|---|---|
| ABC | I'm A Little Teapot | Twinkle Twinkle Little Star |
| Bingo | It's A Small World | We Are The Champions |
| Crocodile Rock | Itsy Bitsy Spider | We Will Rock You |
| Eye Of The Tiger | Just The Way You Are | Yankee Doodle |
| Fearless | Macarena | Yellow Submarine |
| Fireflies | Mary Had A Little Lamb | You Belong With Me |
| Firework | Never Say Never | |
| Hickory Dickory Dock | Old McDonald Had A Farm | |
| Hokey Pokey | Paparazzi | |
| How To Save A Life | Ring Around The Rosie | |
| I Gotta Feeling | Row Row Row Your Boat | |
| | The Lion Sleeps Tonight | |
| | Three Blind Mice | |

# Substitute some words to make this a song about your Hero!

# Try this using another song!

# How do you keep in touch with your Hero?

Phone Calls?

Emails?

SKYPE™

Skype?

Send drawings and pictures?

Videos?

# Make a list of things to talk about next time your Hero calls or Skypes!

School

abc

Pets

Sports

New and Old Friends

_____

_____

_____

_____

_____

_____

_____

_____

_____

# Write a letter to your Hero!

Write about what you've been doing, how much you love your Hero, and how proud you are of him or her.

Ask a grown-up to help you cut this page.

_____

_____

_____

_____

_____

_____

_____

_____

_____

_____

_____

_____ *more room on the back*

When you're done writing your letter, ask a grown-up to
help you cut out this page, and send the letter to your Hero!

# Use this page if you want to write more.

_____

_____

_____

_____

_____

_____

_____

_____

_____

_____

_____

_____

_____

_____ more room on the back

_____

_____

_____

_____

_____

_____

_____

_____

_____

_____

_____

_____

_____

_____

_____

_____

When you're done writing your letter, ask a grown-up to
help you cut out this page, and send the letter to your Hero!

# Getting ready for your Hero to COME BACK HOME!!!

What will change in your life when your Hero returns home?

☆ Cleaning house ☐ more ... ☐ less frequently?

☆ Bedtime will be ☐ later ... ☐ earlier?

☆ Different food for ☐ lunch ... ☐ dinner?

☆ ☐ More chores? ... ☐ Fewer chores?

☆ ☐ More hugs? ... ☐ More games?

## How have YOU changed and what's new about YOU since your Hero has been gone?

_____     _____

_____     _____

_____     _____

_____     _____

_____     _____

# How will you have to act differently when your Hero returns home?

Be on your best behavior.

Give your Hero lots of hugs and kisses.

No loud noises or surprises.

Give your Hero extra space and time alone if he or she needs it.

# How will your Hero have to adjust when he or she returns home?

By seeing
how much you've
grown and changed.

By telling you
what has changed about
himself or herself!

By considering
the whole family when
making decisions.

By getting back
into the
family routine!

Can you think of other ways your Hero might have to adjust once he or she is back home?

_____

_____

_____

_____

_____

_____

# How can you help your Hero when he or she returns home?

By writing a schedule so your Hero knows what to expect.

| | Monday - Friday | Saturday | Sunday |
|---|---|---|---|
| 6 am - 9 am | | | |
| 9 am - 11 am | | | |
| 11 am - 1 pm | | | |
| 1 pm - 3 pm | | | |
| 3 pm - 5 pm | | | |
| 5 pm - 7 pm | | | |
| 7 pm - Bedtime | | | |

NEW RULES

By explaining any new rules since your Hero has been away!

## What else can you think of that might help your Hero?

_____

_____

_____

_____

_____

# Write down the first thing you will do when you see your Hero again!

# Draw a picture of what it will be like to have your Hero back home!

# Send us your drawings, poems, songs, stories, thoughts and letters!

Ask a grown-up to help you email: mystory@rainbowreach.com
or send snail mail to:
Rainbow Reach, 2340 Bedfordshire Circle, Reston, VA 20191

We'll add your materials to our website!*

Send a scan!

Send a photo of your work!

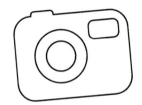

Send original artwork!
If you would like original artwork returned,
please include a self-addressed, stamped envelope.

Include as much (or as little) information as you like ...
name (full name or first name only), age, and what your story is about.

Show and tell us how you are dealing with your difficult situation
and we will share it to help other children.

# Free Drawing Page

Use these extra pages to draw pictures or write your thoughts and feelings. Fill them in now, or use them later when you are thinking about your Hero!

# Free Journal Page

# Free Drawing Page

# Free Journal Page

# Free Drawing Page

# Free Journal Page

# Free Drawing Page

# Free Journal Page

# Free Drawing Page

Free Drawing Page

# Free Journal Page

CPSIA information can be obtained at www.ICGtesting.com
Printed in the USA
BVOW03s0526030916

460759BV00006B/47/P

9 780982 949023